ODD ADAPTATIONS

WHY DO FUNGI FEED ON DEAD PLANTS?

AND OTHER ODD FUNGI ADAPTATIONS

BY JANEY LEVY

Gareth Stevens
PUBLISHING

Please visit our website, www.garethstevens.com. For a free color catalog of all our high-quality books, call toll free 1-800-542-2595 or fax 1-877-542-2596.

Library of Congress Cataloging-in-Publication Data

Names: Levy, Janey, author.
Title: Why do fungi feed on dead plants? : and other odd fungi adaptations / Janey Levy.
Description: New York : Gareth Stevens Publishing, [2019] | Series: Odd adaptations | Includes bibliographical references and index.
Identifiers: LCCN 2017054325| ISBN 9781538220191 (library bound) | ISBN 9781538220214 (pbk.) | ISBN 9781538220221 (6 pack)
Subjects: LCSH: Fungi–Juvenile literature. | Adaptation (Biology)–Juvenile literature.
Classification: LCC QK603.5 .L48 2018 | DDC 579.5–dc23 LC record available at https://lccn.loc.gov/2017054325
First Edition

Published in 2019 by
Gareth Stevens Publishing
111 East 14th Street, Suite 349
New York, NY 10003

Copyright © 2019 Gareth Stevens Publishing

Designer: Sarah Liddell
Editor: Therese Shea

Photo credits: Cover, p. 1 Sanit Fuangnakhon/Shutterstock.com; background used throughout Captblack76/Shutterstock.com; p. 4 vitals/Shutterstock.com; p. 5 Arterra/Contributor/Universal Images Group/Getty Images; p. 6 (morel) JIANG HONGYAN/Shutterstock.com; p. 6 (puffballs) Tamara Kushch/Shutterstock.com; p. 6 (truffle) Radoslav Kellner/Shutterstock.com; p. 7 The Asahi Shimbun/Contributor/The Asahi Shimbun/Getty Images; p. 8 (strawberry) Sumate Chimyindee/Shutterstock.com; p. 8 (bread) schankz/Shutterstock.com; p. 9 DEA/S. VANNINI/Contributor/De Agostini/Getty Images; p. 11 Henry Oude Egberink/Shutterstock.com; p. 12 Sandra Standbridge/Shutterstock.com; p. 13 dcwcreations/Shutterstock.com; p. 14 Kanjanee Chaisin/Shutterstock.com; p. 15 Rodrigo Bellizzi/Shutterstock.com; p. 16 Richard Bradford/Shutterstock.com; p. 17 De Agostini/R. Ostuni/De Agostini Picture Library/Getty Images; p. 18 raimond klavins/Shutterstock.com; p. 19 Gregory MD./Science Source/Getty Images; p. 21 Beta commandBot/Wikimedia Commons; p. 22 Ivan Marjanovic/Shutterstock.com; p. 23 Flickr upload bot/Wikimedia Commons; p. 24 TalyaPhoto/Shutterstock.com; p. 25 (top) NawlinWiki/Wikimedia Commons; p. 25 (middle) Nirajdude/Wikimedia Commons; p. 25 (bottom) File Upload Bot (Magnus Manske)/Wikimedia Commons; p. 26 SCIENCE SOURCE/Science Source/Getty Images; p. 27 BIOPHOTO ASSOCIATES/Science Source/Getty Images; p. 28 Roblan/Shutterstock.com; p. 29 Photo Credit John Dreyer/Moment Open/Getty Images.

All rights reserved. No part of this book may be reproduced in any form without permission in writing from the publisher, except by a reviewer.

Printed in the United States of America

CPSIA compliance information: Batch #CS18GS: For further information contact Gareth Stevens, New York, New York at 1-800-542-2595.

CONTENTS

Fungus Among Us 4

Familiar Fungi 6

Fungi That Feed on Dead Things 10

Freeloading Fungi 14

Zombie-Making Fungi! 18

Friendly Fungi 20

Lovely Lichens 24

Fierce Fungi 26

Fantastic Fungi 28

Glossary 30

For More Information 31

Index 32

Words in the glossary appear in **bold** type the first time they are used in the text.

FUNGUS AMONG US

They're in soil, water, and even the air—but they're often too small to see. Fungi are everywhere! **SCIENTISTS THINK ABOUT 1.5 MILLION SPECIES, OR KINDS, OF FUNGI EXIST.** These odd organisms are necessary for life on Earth!

Fungi have a body called the mycelium (my-SEE-lee-uhm) that's composed of thin threads called hyphae (HY-fee). But that body rarely can be seen. It's commonly hidden in soil or some food source. Fungi reproduce using **spores**, which often come from a visible part called a fruiting body. All the adaptations that fungi have **evolved**—their forms and ways of life—are wonderfully odd.

PLANT OR ANIMAL?

Fungi were once grouped with plants, but scientists now put them in their own kingdom. Why? **ADAPTATIONS MAKE FUNGI LIKE PLANTS IN SOME WAYS AND LIKE ANIMALS IN OTHER WAYS.** They can't make their own food, like plants do, but must get it from other organisms, like animals do. Check out the table on the next page to learn more.

THREE KINGDOMS

FUNGI	PLANTS	ANIMALS
• ARE MADE UP OF MANY CELLS • HAVE CELL WALLS MADE OF TOUGH MATTER CALLED CHITIN • ARE UNABLE TO MOVE • GET **NUTRIENTS** FROM OTHER ORGANISMS • STORE ENERGY AS GLYCOGEN	• ARE MADE UP OF MANY CELLS • HAVE CELL WALLS MADE OF MATTER CALLED CELLULOSE • ARE USUALLY UNABLE TO MOVE • MAKE THEIR OWN FOOD • STORE ENERGY AS STARCH	• ARE MADE UP OF MANY CELLS • HAVE CELLS BUT LACK CELL WALLS • ARE ABLE TO MOVE • GET NUTRIENTS FROM OTHER ORGANISMS • STORE EXTRA ENERGY AS GLYCOGEN

A FRUITING BODY IS THE FRUIT OF THE FUNGUS, JUST LIKE THE APPLE IS THE FRUIT OF THE APPLE TREE. A MUSHROOM IS A FAMILIAR FRUITING BODY.

HYPHAE

FAMILIAR FUNGI

Let's start our exploration of the fungi kingdom with those familiar fungi, mushrooms. True mushrooms are the visible, umbrella-shaped fruiting bodies of certain fungi. Their job is to release, or let out, spores—sometimes hundreds of millions per hour. The spores come from thin, bladelike **gills** or tiny holes called pores, both located on the underside of the cap.

MUSHROOMS' UNDERGROUND MYCELIA HAVE A REMARKABLE ADAPTATION: THEY CAN LIVE HUNDREDS OF YEARS IF THEY HAVE A SUFFICIENT FOOD SUPPLY!

And they'll produce new mushrooms annually during their fruiting season as long as there's food and the correct temperature and moisture.

SOME FUNGI THAT AREN'T TRUE MUSHROOMS ARE STILL WIDELY CONSIDERED MUSHROOMS. THESE INCLUDE PUFFBALLS, MORELS, AND TRUFFLES.

PUFFBALLS

MOREL

TRUFFLE

GLOWING MUSHROOMS

Some mushrooms in the Brazilian rainforest have a surprising adaptation. **THEY'RE BIOLUMINESCENT!** That means they have a chemical inside them that makes them glow. But what's the purpose? Scientists think the glow draws the types of insects and other animals that help spread the mushrooms' spores around the forest.

Other familiar fungi are molds. You've probably encountered molds at home. They've adapted to feed on many different food sources. Some feed on fruits and bread, causing them to look hairy or fuzzy, and spoil. Yuck! Why do molds look the way they do? It's because you're seeing the hyphae. Molds don't produce fruiting bodies like mushrooms. Instead, some of their hyphae produce their spores.

SOME MOLDS ARE ADAPTED TO GROW AND FEED ON "DEAD" MATTER SUCH AS THE WALLS OF YOUR HOUSE. This is particularly true in damp, or moist, areas such as bathrooms, basements, or rooms that have been flooded. People often call these kinds of mold "mildew."

LIFESAVING MOLD

Has penicillin ever helped make you well? If it did, you can thank a mold! Alexander Fleming discovered penicillin by accident in 1928 when he was studying bacteria. **HE NOTICED SOME MOLD HAD POLLUTED ONE DISH—AND STOPPED THE GROWTH OF THE BACTERIA!** Fleming's discovery led to the creation of penicillin, the first antibiotic.

SOMETIMES, MOLD ON FOOD IS CONSIDERED A GOOD THING. MOLD IS USED TO MAKE SOFT CHEESES SUCH AS BRIE AND CAMEMBERT.

FUNGI THAT FEED ON DEAD THINGS

Now that we've gotten acquainted with some of the basic features of fungi, let's look at the main categories, or classes. We'll start with saprophytic (saa-pruh-FIH-tihk) fungi—those fungi that feed on dead organic matter. These include most mushrooms.

Since saprophytic fungi can't move, it makes sense that dead matter would be a great food source for them. Dead matter doesn't move, either. But fungi—all fungi—have no mouth or stomach. So what adaptations have they evolved to help them "eat"? **FUNGI RELEASE ENZYMES THAT DIGEST FOOD OUTSIDE THEIR BODY.** Then the fungi absorb, or take in, the nutrients!

BREAK IT DOWN

When saprophytic fungi are digesting dead organic matter, they're breaking it down. Their purpose is to gain nutrients, but they're also performing an important service. **IF FUNGI DIDN'T BREAK DOWN LEAVES, TWIGS, AND EVEN LOGS, THAT DEAD MATTER WOULD PILE UP ON THE FOREST FLOOR INTO ENORMOUS, TOWERING HEAPS.**

When saprophytic fungi digest dead matter, they're freeing up nutrients—and not just for themselves. They're actually recycling those nutrients, returning them to the soil, and making the soil richer. The nutrients can then be used by other living organisms. Without the fungi's recycling work, the nutrients would remain locked up in the dead matter.

The fungi's job in breaking down dead wood is especially important. **WOOD HAS LIGNIN, THE MATTER THAT MAKES IT STIFF. ANIMALS CAN'T DIGEST LIGNIN, BUT CERTAIN SAPROPHYTIC FUNGI ARE ADAPTED TO.** They keep all the dead wood in the forest from piling up.

SPREADING SPORES

Saprophytic fungi, like all fungi, want to spread, or disperse, their spores, but a layer of still air near the ground makes that hard. Fungi have several adaptations to deal with the problem. **STINKHORNS, FOR EXAMPLE, DRAW FLIES WITH THEIR ROTTEN-MEAT SMELL.** Spores stick to the flies, which carry them away.

STINKHORN

IF SAPROPHYTIC FUNGI DIDN'T DO THEIR RECYCLING WORK, SOIL WOULD SLOWLY BECOME LESS RICH AND FEWER PLANTS WOULD GROW.

FREELOADING FUNGI

Some fungi are parasites. They feed off living plant and animal **hosts** and harm those hosts, sometimes killing them.

Humans are often affected by certain parasitic fungi, and you or someone you know might have suffered from fungal problems. One common condition caused by parasitic fungi is athlete's foot. The fungus that usually causes athlete's foot is *Trichophyton rubrum*. **IT HAS ADAPTED SO ITS SPORES SURVIVE FOR 12 MONTHS IN FLAKES OF SKIN THAT HAVE FALLEN OFF THE BODY.** That means it's easily spread from person to person in places such as the gym. That's why it's called athlete's foot!

ATHLETE'S FOOT MAY BE DRY, RED, AND ITCHY OR MOIST, WHITE, AND PEELING. EITHER WAY, IT'S NOT A PLEASANT EXPERIENCE!

ATHLETE'S FOOT

CIRCLES AND RINGS

Another common fungal condition is ringworm. In spite of the name, it's caused by a group of fungi called dermatophytes (duhr-MAA-tuh-fyts), not a worm. **THESE FUNGI ARE ADAPTED TO FEED ON KERATIN, A PROTEIN THAT MAKES UP MOST OF THE OUTERMOST LAYER OF SKIN AS WELL AS THE HAIR AND NAILS.**

Parasitic fungi cause many plant diseases, or sicknesses, that harm and often kill the plants. Dutch elm disease is one such sickness. **THE FUNGI THAT CAUSE THE DISEASE HAVE A SPECIAL ADAPTATION: THEY USE BEETLES TO SPREAD FROM SICK TREES TO HEALTHY TREES.** Hundreds of thousands of elm trees have been killed in the United States in the last 90 years.

Another common parasitic fungus is honey fungus, a name that's applied to several different *Armillaria* species. It attacks all kinds of trees. It has adapted to spread from tree to tree underground, through bundles of hyphae called rhizomorphs (RY-zuh-mohrfs).

AN ANCIENT GIANT

It may be hard to believe this is true of a fungus, but an *Armillaria ostoyae* discovered in Oregon in 1998 is one of the largest organisms in the world. How big is it? It occupies about 2,385 acres (965 ha). It's also very old. **SCIENTISTS THINK IT'S BETWEEN 2,400 AND 8,650 YEARS OLD!**

Armillaria rhizomorphs grow under the bark of a tree and may finally cause the bark to fall off. They rot wood, slow growth, and finally kill the tree.

ZOMBIE-MAKING FUNGI!

SOME PARASITIC FUNGI HAVE AN ADAPTATION RIGHT OUT OF A HORROR MOVIE: THEY TURN THEIR HOSTS INTO ZOMBIES THAT DO THEIR BIDDING! These fungi, species of *Ophiocordyceps*, live in **tropical** rain forests. By themselves, they're not able to reach the leaves that are their ideal home. So they create zombie ants to take them there.

Spores **infect** an ant's brain, forcing the ant to leave its colony, go to a leaf that meets the fungus's requirements, bite down, and die. The fungus then grows inside the ant's body and finally pushes a fruiting body up through the ant's head. It rains down spores, infecting ants below.

OPHIOCORDYCEPS SINENSIS

CATERPILLAR FUNGUS

The species called *Ophiocordyceps sinensis* does strange things to some caterpillars in parts of China. The spores infect the caterpillar, then the hyphae grow inside it. The caterpillar dies, and the fungus's mycelium takes on the shape of the caterpillar's body. Finally, the fungus puts up a fruiting body that looks like a dry stick.

This image shows a dead zombie ant with the fungus's fruiting body sticking out of its head. Ants infected with these fungi always bite the underside of a leaf.

FRIENDLY FUNGI

Some fungi have a symbiotic (sihm-bee-AH-tihk) relationship with plants. That is, they have a relationship in which everyone benefits: The fungi get something from the plants, and the plants get something from the fungi.

SEVERAL FUNGI ARE ADAPTED TO FORM AN ASSOCIATION, OR CONNECTION, WITH PLANTS BY JOINING WITH THE PLANTS' ROOTS. The association is called mycorrhiza (my-kuh-RY-zuh). Sometimes the hyphae of a fungus wrap around the roots of a plant. Other times, the hyphae actually pierce the roots. The fungus acquires sugars from the plant. In exchange, the plant gets nutrients the fungus draws from the soil that the plant's roots can't reach.

FUNGI VS. FUNGI

Symbiotic fungi can benefit their hosts in other ways as well. They protect their hosts from parasitic fungi. They may attack the parasitic fungi, or they may simply take up so much space there's no room for parasitic fungi to grow. **MYCORRHIZAL FUNGI KEEP THEIR COMPANION PLANTS HEALTHIER AND BETTER ABLE TO RESIST DISEASE.**

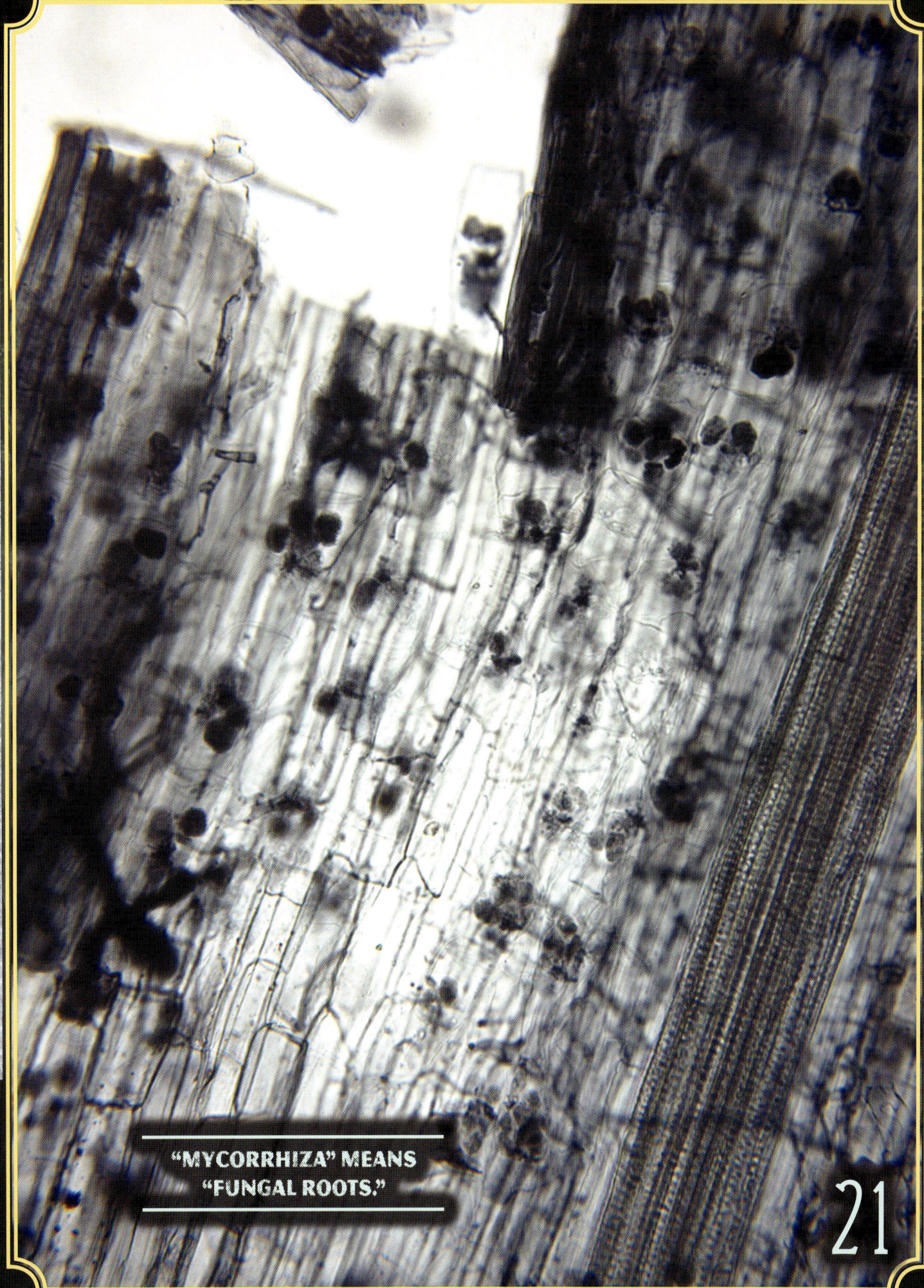

"MYCORRHIZA" MEANS "FUNGAL ROOTS."

How important are mycorrhizal fungi? **THEY'VE ADAPTED TO THEIR JOB SO WELL THAT ABOUT 90 PERCENT OF LAND PLANTS DEPEND ON THEM!** During winter, when days are shorter and there's less sunlight, some plants can't produce enough food and wouldn't survive without their fungi. Mycorrhizal fungi are especially important in nutrient-poor soils. Some plants, such as orchids, can't grow without these fungi.

In some forests, there are so many mycorrhizal fungi that their mycelia actually connect the trees. **THE MYCELIA ARE ADAPTED TO ACT AS A KIND OF INTERNET FOR THE TREES, EXCHANGING NUTRIENTS AND CHEMICAL MESSAGES.**

AURICULARIA

TRUFFLES ARE MYCORRHIZAL FUNGI. SO IS *AURICULARIA*, THE MUSHROOM USED TO FLAVOR THE POPULAR CHINESE SWEET-AND-SOUR SOUP.

ANCIENT EARTH

Since almost all land plants depend on mycorrhizal fungi, scientists think the fungi may have been necessary for plants to move from the ocean to land millions of years ago. In fact, a 440-million-year-old fungus may be the oldest fossilized land organism ever found!

HYACINTH ORCHID

LOVELY LICHENS

Lichens (LY-kuhnz) represent a symbiotic relationship between one or two fungus species and an **alga** or a **cyanobacterium**. But it's an unusual relationship: Unlike most symbiotic relationships, it results in an individual, new form with its own name—lichen.

LICHENS' ADAPTATIONS HAVE MADE THEM EXTREMELY STURDY ORGANISMS THAT GROW ON ALMOST ANY SURFACE AND CAN BE FOUND ALMOST EVERYWHERE, INCLUDING WHERE FEW PLANTS SURVIVE. They grow farther north and south on Earth and higher on mountains than most plants. Some are even found near the North and South Poles!

YOU MAY HAVE SEEN LICHENS GROWING ON TREES OR ROCKS.

WET AND DRY

Lichens make more food when they're moist. However, they quickly lose water vapor they've absorbed from the air and have no way to absorb water from the surface they're attached to. **YOU MIGHT THINK BEING DRY WOULD BE BAD, BUT IT'S ACTUALLY A PROTECTIVE ADAPTATION.** Dry lichen is more resistant to temperature and light extremes.

FUNGI CATEGORIES

SAPROPHYTIC FUNGI
FEED ON DEAD THINGS
EXAMPLES: MUSHROOMS, STINKHORNS

PARASITIC FUNGI
FEED ON LIVING PLANT AND ANIMAL HOSTS AND HARM THEM
EXAMPLES: ATHLETE'S FOOT, RINGWORM, ZOMBIE-MAKING FUNGI

SYMBIOTIC FUNGI
LIVE IN RELATIONSHIP WITH HOST IN WHICH EVERYONE BENEFITS
EXAMPLES: MYCORRHIZAL FUNGI, LICHEN

FIERCE FUNGI

This just might be the oddest, creepiest fungus adaptation of all: **SOME FUNGI ARE PREDATORS!** That might be hard to imagine for an unmoving organism with no mouth, but these fungi capture and eat small worms called nematodes as well as other tiny organisms.

Predatory fungi have several ways to capture nematodes. Some produce hyphae ending in rings that tighten when a nematode moves through them. Then they pierce the nematode with a hypha to kill it. Other fungi make hyphae covered with a sort of sticky glue to trap nematodes. They pierce the stuck nematode or make a poison to kill it.

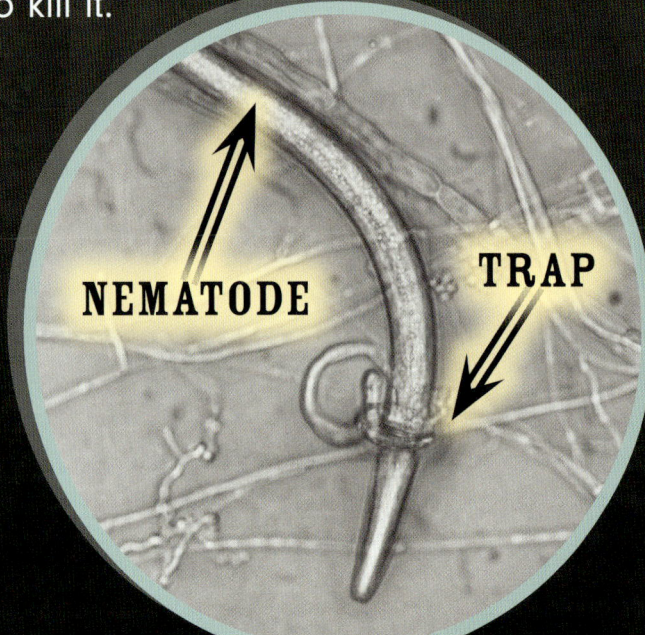

NEMATODE — TRAP

ON THE HUNT

Making traps to catch nematodes uses a lot of energy, so predatory fungi don't want to do it unless they know nematodes are around. But how can they know if nematodes are around? **THE FUNGI HAVE ADAPTED TO BE ABLE TO DETECT CERTAIN CHEMICALS THE NEMATODES RELEASE.**

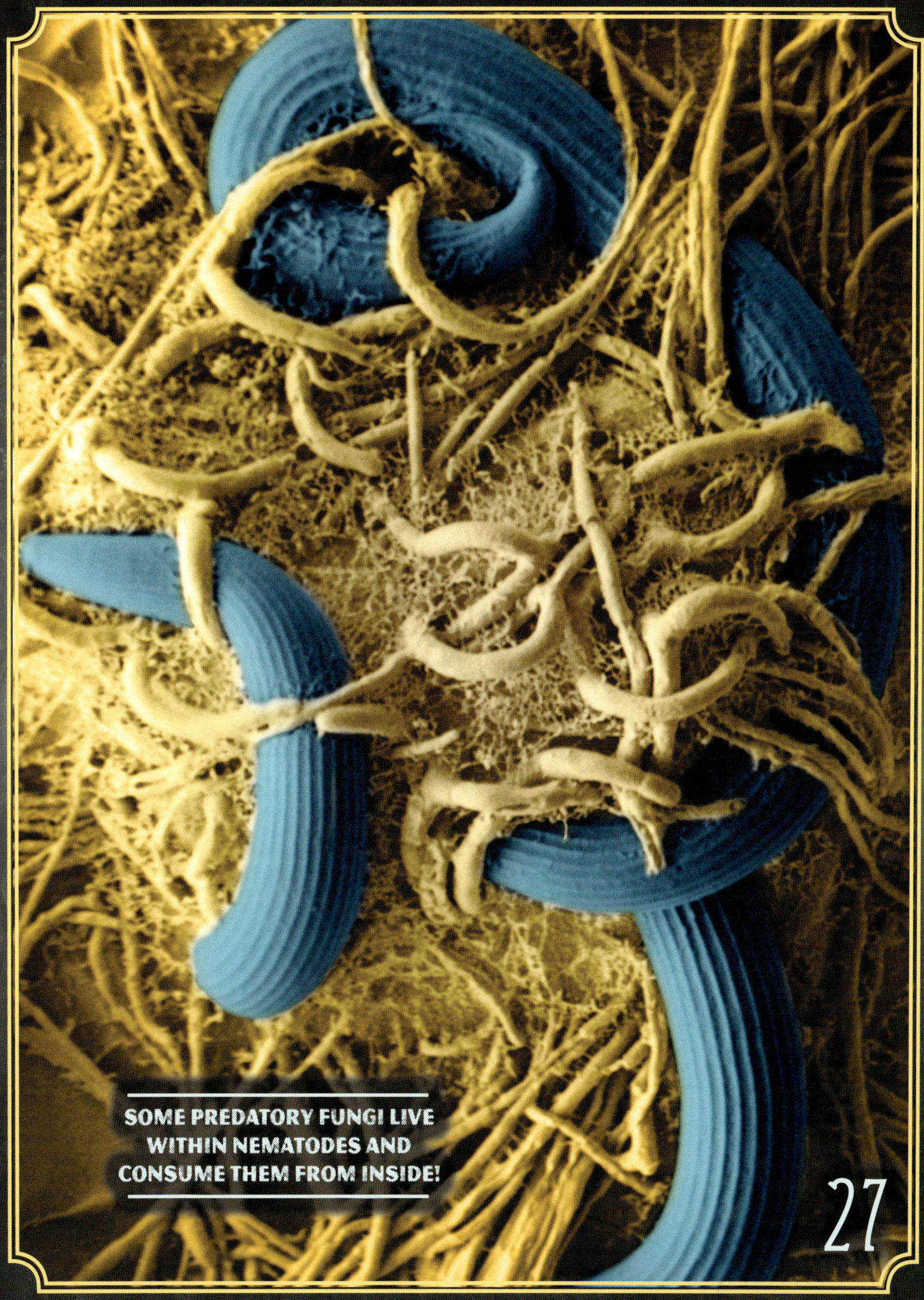

FANTASTIC FUNGI

FUNGI FRUITING BODIES ARE IMPORTANT PARTS OF FOREST FOOD WEBS. Squirrels store them to eat through the winter. The teeth marks of other small forest animals are often found on mushroom caps.

Fungi's adaptations have allowed them to do amazing things. Yes, some are parasites, but most are helpful. They break down dead matter and recycle nutrients. They form mycorrhizal relationships with plants that keep plants healthy. In fact, they may have made it possible for plants to live on land. And without plants on land, we wouldn't be here. Fungi make life on Earth possible!

YUMMY YEASTS

Besides the fungi in this book, many more kinds exist thanks to odd and amazing adaptations. **YEASTS, FOR EXAMPLE, DON'T HAVE A MYCELIUM: THEY'VE ADAPTED TO GROW AS SINGLE CELLS, AND MANY REPRODUCE BY BUDDING.** They're found everywhere in soil, flower nectar, and fruit. People use yeasts to make bread and wine.

YEAST

FUNGI ALSO PROVIDE FOOD AND HOMES FOR ALL SORTS OF INSECTS AND THEIR LARVAE.

GLOSSARY

alga: a living plantlike thing that is mostly found in water

bud: to produce a new cell by pinching off a small part of the parent cell

cyanobacterium: any one of a group of bacteria that are able to make their own food, like plants do

digest: to break down food inside the body so that the body can use it

enzyme: a protein made in the body that helps chemical reactions occur

evolve: to grow and change over time

gill: one of the thin, bladelike plates that produce spores, located on the underside of the cap of true mushrooms

host: an organism in which another organism lives and gets its food

infect: to cause to become sick or filled with something harmful

nutrient: something a living thing needs to grow and stay alive

protein: a nutrient in many types of food that an organism uses to grow, repair itself, and stay healthy

spore: a small body made by a fungus that can grow into another fungus

tropical: having to do with the warm parts of Earth near the equator

FOR MORE INFORMATION

BOOKS

Billups, Carla, and Dawn Cusick. *It's a Fungus Among Us: The Good, the Bad and the Downright Scary.* Lake Forest, CA: MoonDance Press, 2017.

Wearing, Judy. *Fungi: Mushrooms, Toadstools, Molds, Yeasts, and Other Fungi.* New York, NY: Crabtree Publishing, 2010.

WEBSITES

Fungi
www.ducksters.com/science/biology/fungi.php
Read more about fungi here and take a short quiz.

Fungi Facts
www.softschools.com/facts/biology/fungi_facts/2515/
Find some interesting facts about fungi on this site.

Publisher's note to educators and parents: Our editors have carefully reviewed these websites to ensure that they are suitable for students. Many websites change frequently, however, and we cannot guarantee that a site's future contents will continue to meet our high standards of quality and educational value. Be advised that students should be closely supervised whenever they access the internet.

INDEX

alga 25

bioluminescence 7

cyanobacterium 25

Dutch elm disease 16

Fleming, Alexander 8

gills 6

hyphae 4, 8, 16, 18, 20, 26

kingdoms 5

lichen 24, 25

mold 8, 9

mushroom 5, 6, 7, 8, 10, 22, 25, 28

mycelium 4, 18

mycorrhizal fungi 20, 21, 22, 23, 25, 28

Ophiocordyceps 18

parasites 14

penicillin 8

rhizomorphs 16, 17

ringworm 15, 25

saprophytic fungi 10, 12, 13, 26

spores 4, 6, 9, 12, 13, 14, 18

Trichophyton rubrum (athlete's foot) 14, 26